Intermittent Fasting
for Women Over 50

How to Eat Healthy, Lose Weight and Improve Your Life with Intermittent Fasting. The Guide to Master All the benefits of Fasting, Promote Longevity and Detoxify the Body

Patricia Emmerich

TABLE OF CONTENT

INTRODUCTION

Intermittent fasting is the practice of assigning time periods during which you will eat (eating window) and time periods during which you will not eat (fasting window). Those are the two most important factors to consider when practicing intermittent fasting. The regime does not dictate what you should eat. If you are undertaking fasting to lose weight you would need to restrict your calorie intake. Overall a healthy diet of lean protein with plenty of fresh fruit and vegetables is ideal for fasting. Processed foods should be avoided even if you are not practicing intermittent fasting as they are extremely unhealthy and can damage your body. During the fasting period, nothing with a calorie content should be consumed. You can (and should) consume beverages during your fasting window but these should be limited to water or tea and coffee without additives such as milk and sugar. It is actually very important to ensure that you remain hydrated while you fast as much of the liquid we take in is in food. Water is your best option for this and if you don't like the taste of plain water you can infuse it with lemon, lime, mint or cucumber which does not add calories.

Intermittent fasting is not starvation, by any means. The term starvation refers to a forced situation in which there is no access to food and the body experiences highly damaging side effects from lack of nutrition. If anything, fasting is the opposite of starvation as you are choosing not to eat during your fasting window and rather than causing damage, fasting actually works to repair and help improve your body's natural process and responses.

One of the biggest differences between these two concepts is your mindset. Intermittent fasting is about breathing life back into your body and giving it the opportunity to accelerate its processes and improve the way it naturally heals.

Fasting has been around for millennia. It has played important roles in religious and medical literature for nearly as long. In many modern religions, fasting is the way to create spiritual connection, to find guidance or to improve mindfulness. Fasts that automatically come to mind are Lent in Catholic and Orthodox Christianity, Ramadan in Islam or meditation fasts is some Buddhist schools. Lent lasts 40 days, and while some churches may allow more freedom with the fast, traditionally Lent required a fast where only one meal a day was eaten. During Ramadan, a month long fast, Muslims don't eat while the sun is up and then eaten once the sun is down. Essentially, it is an eight to 12 hour fast, with some time to eat at night and early in the morning. In some Buddhist schools, fasting takes place to aid in meditation and spiritual practices. This often happens every day, with the dinner meal skipped. So, within religions and spiritual practices, there are many different kinds of fasts.

People have also fasted for political reasons. Perhaps most famously is Gandhi and his social protests. He fasted multiple times to protest a variety of social issues in India. There have been other hunger-strikes throughout history, where people fasted to create political change including suffragette fasting in Europe and the U.S. Many political fasts promote a feeling of guilt in those watching, and can result in change, though it has often resulted in death as well.

Medically, fasting has been around since the time of Hippocrates. Fasting was prescribed during times when the patient was sick enough that eating was considered detrimental. Past physicians believed that fasting would help with the healing of injuries and diseases. While it's unclear whether this was actually true, today, modern fasting is associated with better health improvements. In fact, intermittent fasting is our modern take on fasting for healing.

Intermittent fasting is when you choose not to eat for a specific amount of time. For example, you might fast during the evening and night hours, or you might fast every other day. In general, intermittent fasting doesn't go beyond a day of fasting. So, you won't see many intermittent fasts that are 30 hours of fasting or longer. Despite how it may sound, intermittent fasting is not starvation and in fact, it's quite healthy. Intermittent fasts are about improving your health. In general, it can benefit people who are looking to lose weight, improve their blood sugar levels, and reduce their insulin resistance.

HOW INTERMITTENT FASTING WORKS?

As with any lifestyle change, intermittent fasting may be difficult at first. You may experience some irritability or a drop in energy. You may feel really hungry and have a hard time sticking to your plan. Or you might feel great right off the bat, experiencing positive results immediately and feeling energized and motivated by your new lifestyle. It depends on your body. However, there are some things that are likely to occur as you adjust to your new routine. When you know what to expect, and you have some tools ready to cope with any challenges that may arise, your chances for long-term success are much greater.

How Your Mind Will Feel

There's a popular quote that says, "Your mind will quit a thousand times before your body will," and another quote that states, "Your body can stand almost anything. It's your mind you have to convince." The general message behind both of these powerful quotes is that often, when you give up, it's not because you've actually reached your physical limit, it's because you've reached your mental limit. In other words, your mind convinces you that your body can't physically handle a challenge when it actually can.

Negativity Bias

Your brain has a tendency to react more strongly to negative things than it does to positive things. This phenomenon is called the negativity bias-and it can be extremely powerful. The biological purpose of the negativity bias is to protect you from possible threats, but in modern times, threats like those faced by your ancestors are fewer and farther between. As a result, you don't need this negativity bias as often, because it's not as helpful as it once was. In fact, this bias makes it harder for you to be present and calm because you're always on alert and anticipating a negative event instead of appreciating the moment. The good news is that you can actually retrain your brain so that it doesn't revert to the negativity bias as easily.

Positive Thinking

Positive thinking and affirmations are not just New Age trends: they're powerful tools that can actually rewire the neurons in your brain-a concept known as neuroplasticity. When you regularly engage in positive thinking and repeat positive affirmations, it makes it easier for your brain to respond more positively to things rather than immediately resorting to its natural negativity bias. And the more you practice, the easier it becomes for your brain to think positively.

When you're starting out with intermittent fasting, your subconscious mind will resist the change and will do all it can to get you to resort back to your old routine. When you know this, it's easier to become aware of negative thought patterns and unconstructive self-talk. You may find yourself thinking things like, "This is way too hard," "I'm starving," or "A small snack outside of my fasting window won't hurt." These thoughts are all indications that your negativity bias is running the show.

When your mind starts to tell you that it's too hard, recognize that it is this bias talking and respond by saying something like, "I'm stronger than my thoughts. I can and will meet my goals." Neuroplasticity refers to the brain's ability to change and adapt to an environment. The brain goes through physiological changes from the day you are born to the end of your life. Neurogenesis is the formation of new brain cells. Like neuroplasticity, neurogenesis also happens throughout your life but only in certain areas of the brain. In addition to regularly practicing positive affirmations and changing your negative self-talk, you can also shut your negativity bias down by focusing on the bigger picture.

Figure out your main reasons for fasting. Is it to lose weight? Gain more mental clarity and energy? Balance your blood sugar levels? Keep your brain healthy? Whatever your reasons are, write them on a piece of paper or sticky notes and keep them somewhere you will see them frequently, like on the refrigerator. When you feel these negative thoughts start to creep in, read the notes, and remember your main goals and why you started in the first place. This can help you see the bigger picture, which will get you through any little speed bumps along the way. Once you get past the initial stages of intermittent fasting, it's likely that you'll notice some major changes.

Not only will your negative self-talk and negativity bias diminish, but you'll also experience more mental clarity. Intermittent fasting tends to lift brain fog and make concentration easier. You may find that simple tasks become easier and that you're able to focus on your work more. You may also experience less "monkey mind"-intrusive, rapid thoughts that distract you from the task at hand and interfere with your productivity. You may notice your productivity and energy levels increasing. Your memory may feel sharper and retaining new information may become easier than it was before. You may also notice a stabilization in your moods and emotions-even less anxiety and a more cheerful disposition.

How Your Body Will Feel

It's impossible to say exactly how your body will feel during the initial stages of intermittent fasting, since everyone is different, and you may respond differently than someone else. However, there are a few things that commonly occur in most people when starting intermittent fasting. If you're used to eating five or six times per day, you may experience these effects to a greater degree than if you already eat three meals a day with minimal snacking. As your body adjusts to intermittent fasting, it's normal to feel increased hunger and cravings. Often this is mental or emotional hunger rather than physical hunger. You may also experience headaches, low energy, and irritability.

It's possible to feel a little dizzy, weak, or light-headed upon standing. The severity of these symptoms can vary based on several factors, including your previous eating habits, but they shouldn't be extremely intrusive, and they should diminish within a week or so. If you are experiencing severe symptoms that don't go away or improve, discontinue your fast immediately and speak with your healthcare provider. It could be a sign of blood sugar problems that require medical supervision.

After the initial adjustment period, your blood sugar and insulin levels start to stabilize, and you'll begin to reap the benefits of intermittent fasting. One of the first things you'll likely notice is increased energy. You may feel sustained energy throughout the day instead of feeling awake and productive in the morning, but then being hit with that dreaded afternoon slump around two or three p.m.; you'll feel constant energy.

This is because your blood sugar isn't spiking and dropping like it does when you eat several meals over the course of the entire day. You may also experience a decrease in inflammation, so any puffiness in your face, skin, hands, or feet may start to diminish. Chronic aches and pains that became a regular part of your day may reduce or go away completely. Then you might start to notice that you're dropping a few extra pounds, that you fall asleep easier, and that the quality of your sleep is better. You'll toss and turn less at night, and as a result, you'll wake up feeling refreshed and rested instead of groggy and disoriented. If you're exercising regularly, you might also find it easier to get through your workouts.

A good way to keep track of changes is to write down any symptoms you feel before starting your intermittent fasting plan. Try to dig deep and be really comprehensive, even listing things that you've dealt with for a long time or that you think have nothing to do with your eating habits. After you've been fasting for a couple of weeks, go back and rewrite your list and compare the two lists. Rewrite your list every couple of weeks after that. This can help you track improvements that you may not even be expecting, and it's likely that you'll be pleasantly surprised.

Staving Off Hunger

In the initial stages of intermittent fasting, you're going to feel hungry; there's no way around that. Luckily, with an understanding of hunger cues and a few easy techniques, you can stave off both physical and mental hunger without breaking your fast.

The Psychology of Hunger

Hunger is tricky because, on one hand, there's true, physiological hunger; on the other hand, there's mental hunger. Put simply: physical hunger occurs when your stomach is empty. You may feel the physical emptiness in your stomach, along with a weakness or a dip in energy. Psychological hunger is the result of a desire to eat out of habit or boredom or because of external cues. While you may do these things subconsciously, when you become aware of them, you can change how they affect you. Instead of mindlessly eating because you're at a social event or your significant other is hungry, pay attention to how you really feel. Are you truly hungry, or are you just tempted by one of these cues?

Drink Water

During your fasting periods (and in general), water should be your best friend. You've probably heard that thirst is often mistaken for hunger, so staying hydrated can help diminish any false hunger signals. Right when you wake up, drink 8 ounces of water. You can prepare by having a glass of water on your nightstand when you go to sleep. If you exercise a lot or lose sweat in other ways, you may need to drink even more than that. You'll also need to add an extra glass of water for every cup of coffee or other diuretic you drink, so keep that in mind.

Look for (and Eliminate) Triggers

Look for things that trigger your psychological hunger-and then avoid those things. Up until now, you may have been on autopilot when it comes to eating. You haven't really been paying attention to what is going on around you or what is influencing the amount or the types of food you eat. For example, do you have a significant other who eats twice as much as you do? Do you keep your favorite snacks in the pantry or refrigerator within sight every time you open the doors? Do you schedule social events around food?

What kinds of restaurants are you choosing for these events, or what kinds of dishes are you and your friends making? Figuring out the things that trigger you to eat more-or to choose unhealthy foods will go a long way not only in maintaining intermittent fasting as a lifestyle but also in preserving your health. Surround yourself with people who support your lifestyle changes and stay away from-or limit time with people who might sabotage your efforts.

Tips and Tools to Stay Focused

The most important thing you can do to ensure your success with intermittent fasting is to have a plan. The first step is to determine which type of fasting you're going to do. Once you've determined the type of fasting, make a schedule. Are you going to fast every day? What times will you fast, and what times will you feed? After you've developed your timeline, another critical component is determining what you're going to eat when it's time to enter your fed state. Are you going to follow a specific dietary regimen (like the ketogenic diet or Paleo Diet), or are you going to stick to a basic clean-eating plan with no real "rules"?

REASONS YOU SHOULD START INTERMITTENT FASTING TODAY
IF YOU'RE A
WOMAN OVER 50

There are plenty of diets out there, all promising you the impossible. Incredible weight loss, with no mention of any side effects. You are probably fed up with the "lose x pounds in 30 days, guaranteed" approach. Many of these diets are not backed up by science, or in other words, there is not any scientific research to prove these diets actually deliver what they promise. They focus only on the weight loss process, suggesting meal plans that are extremely radical in some cases.

Diets mean nutrient deprivation in most cases, but they are plenty of cases when these diets have harmful effects on your health. Unlike other diets, focused on the weight loss process in an incredibly short amount of time, intermittent fasting is focusing more on your health, as nutritionists believe that health should be the most important factor, and only a healthy body can have a long and sustainable weight loss process. Unlike the other diets, which have a "hit and run" approach, IF is something for the long run and should be regarded as a way of life, not like a meal plan to be implemented for a few weeks. By checking out the benefits below, you can better understand why this process is so beneficial for your body.

The main benefits of intermittent fasting can be summarized in 8 points:

- Eliminates precancerous and cancerous cells
- Shifts easily into nutritional ketosis
- Reduces the fat tissue
- Enhances the gene expression for health span and longevity
- Induces autophagy and the apoptotic cellular repair or cleaning
- Improves your insulin sensitivity
- Reduces inflammation and oxidative stress
- Increases neuroprotection and cognitive effects

To expand on the benefits of this practice, intermittent fasting can have positive impacts over the fat loss process, disease prevention, anti-aging, therapeutic benefits (psychological, spiritual and physical), mental performance, physical fitness (improved metabolism, wind, and endurance, the great effect over bodybuilding).

Healthy Eating Habits

As you restrain yourself from eating, the body will no longer have available glucose to use in order to produce energy. Therefore, it will use ketones to break the fat tissue open and release the energy stored in there. This is how the body will burn your existing fat in order to generate energy. When it comes to diets, they are not designed for the long run, and as soon as you break the diet, you will start gaining weight again. Intermittent fasting is something that you can try for a lifetime because it is easy to stick to it, and it doesn't involve any special meal plan. So, you can still eat your favorite foods, as long as you schedule your meals, allowing a smaller eating window and a longer fasting period. IF induces ketosis and eventually autophagy, which will definitely mean reducing the fat reserves.

Preventing Diseases

What if you found out that intermittent fasting is, in fact, a cure for several different diseases and medical conditions? You would definitely become more interested in this process. There are a few studies that show the beneficial effects IF has on your health. A study published in the World Journal of Diabetes has shown that patients with type 2 diabetes on short-term daily intermittent fasting experience a lower body weight, but also a better variability of post-meal glucose.

Other benefits this diet has are:

- Enhances the markers of stress resistance
- Reduces the blood pressure and inflammation
- Better lipid levels and glucose circulation, which may lead to a lower risk of cardiovascular disease, neurological diseases like Parkinson's and Alzheimer's, and also cancer

Anti-Aging Process

The modern-day lifestyle includes too much stress and is too sedentary. Whether we like it or not, these factors have a great contribution to the aging process. You are probably wondering what intermittent fasting can do the slow down this process, as we all know that it can't be stopped. IF is not "the fountain of youth" and it will not grant you immortality, but it can still lower the blood pressure and reduce oxidative damage, enhance your insulin sensitivity and reduce your fat mass. Coincidence or not, all of these are factors are known to improve your health and longevity. Intermittent fasting is one of the triggering factors of autophagy, a process known for destroying and replacing old cell parts with new ones, at any level within your body. Such a process can slow down the aging process.

Therapeutic Benefits

When it comes to therapeutic benefits, the most important ones are physical, spiritual and psychological. In terms of physical benefits, intermittent fasting is a powerful cure for diabetes, but it can also prove to be very useful for reducing seizure-related brain damage and seizures themselves, but also for improving the symptoms of arthritis. This practice also has a spiritual value, as it's widely practiced for religious purposes across the globe. Although fasting is regarded as penance by some practitioners, it's also a practice for purifying your body and soul (according to the religious approach).

Intermittent fasting is also about exercising control and will, over your body and your feelings. Achieving absolute control over your power and mind is a very powerful psychological benefit. You can ignore hunger, restrain yourself from eating for a certain period of time. In other words, IF is also associated with mind training and can also improve your self-esteem. A successful intermittent fasting regime can have very powerful effects from a psychological point of view. A study has shown that women practicing IF had amazing results in terms of senses of control, reward, pride, and achievement.

Brain Health

IF also enhances the cognitive function and also is very useful when it comes to boosting your brain power. There are several factors of intermittent fasting which can support this claim. First of all, it boosts the level of brain-derived neurotrophic factor (also known as BDNF), which is a protein in your brain that can interact with the parts of your brain responsible for controlling cognitive and memory functions as well as learning. BDNF can even protect and stimulate the growth of new brain cells. Through IF, you will enter the ketogenic state, during which your body turn fat into energy, by using ketones. Ketones can also feed your brain, and therefore improve your mental acuity, productivity, and energy.

Improved Physical Fitness

This process influences not only your brain but also your digestive system. By setting a small feeding window and a larger fasting period, you will encourage the proper digestion of food. This leads to a proportional and healthy daily intake of food and calories. The more you get used to this process, the less you will experience hunger. If you are worried about slowing your metabolism, think again! IF enhances your metabolism, it makes metabolism more flexible, as the body has now the capability to run on glucose or fats for energy, in a very effective way. In other words, intermittent fasting leads to better metabolism.

Oxygen use during exercise is a crucial part of the success of your training. You simply can't have performance without adjusting your breathing habits during workouts. VO2 max represents the maximum amount of oxygen your body can use per minute or per kilogram of body weight. In popular terms, VO2 max is also referred to as "wind". The more oxygen you use, the better you will be able to perform. Top athletes can have twice the VO2 level of those without any training. A study focused on the VO2 levels of a fasted group (they just skipped breakfast) and a non-fasted group (they had breakfasted an hour before). For both groups, the VO2 level was at 3.5 L/min at the beginning, and after the study, the level showed a significant increase of "wind" for the fasting group (9.7%), compared to just 2.5% increase in the case of those with breakfast.

Bodybuilding

Having a narrow feeding window automatically mean fewer meals, so you can concentrate the daily calorie intake into just 1-2 consistent meals. Bodybuilders find this approach a lot more pleasing than having the same calorie consumption split into 5 or 6 different meals throughout the day. It's said that you need a specific amount of proteins just to maintain your muscle mass. However, muscle mass can be also maintained through intermittent fasting, a process which doesn't focus specifically on protein intake. Remember, the growth hormone reaches unbelievable levels after 48 hours of fasting, so you can easily maintain your muscles without eating many proteins or having protein bars or shakes.

As you already know, nothing is perfect and intermittent fasting is no exception. There are a few side effects that you need to worry about, like:

- Hunger is perhaps the most common side effect of this way of eating, but the more you get used to IF, the less hunger you will feel
- Beware of constipation, as when you eat less, you will not have to go to the toilet very often, so you can feel constipated at the beginning
- Headaches should be expected when fasting. Food deprivation is a direct cause of these headaches. However, controlling your hunger and getting used to fasting, will be the best weapon to fight against these headaches

- During intermittent fasting, you might experience muscle cramps, heartburn, and dizziness
- In the case of athletic women, or those with very low body fat percentage, intermittent fasting may lead to a higher risk of irregular periods and lower chances of conception (so it reduces fertility for these women)

WHEN TO AVOID INTERMITTENT FASTING AS A WOMAN

As a woman, you should note that intermittent fasting has become one of the favorite ways of losing weight or even improving your general health. Starvation has been reported to be a fair practice as it positively changes many people's lives. If you have been fasting, you must have heard a notion that fasting is not healthy for women, despite the many positive impacts it has on their bodies. Intermittent fasting has different impacts on men and women. It is less beneficial to women as compared to men.

There exist myths that many women experience changes in their menstrual periods after starting intermittent fasting. These changes may take place since women bodies are reactive, especially after the restriction of calories. When you take fewer calories, the hypothalamus part in the brain is always affected. This means that women should try intermittent fasting with shorter periods. The affected hormones tend to interfere with the ovaries, and that is why the menstrual periods are affected. This brings out the concern of when to avoid intermittent fasting as a woman.

Intermittent Fasting and Menstruation

As recurrent fasting grows into a supplementary general, women who starve on a regular basis might have queries about how starving could impact their multiplicative sequence, hormones and multiplicative well-being. Even though there is some degree of investigation on how recurrent fasting or ketogenic foods may influence multiplicative sequences in persons, you can take some hints from the study including further metabolic and way of life characters and performances such as heaviness, workout and caloric constraint.

Calories constraint, for instance, can be said to be a "stressor" handled in your mind and might as well adjust discharge of gender hormone via an axis known as the "Hypothalamic-Pituitary-Gonadal (HPG)" alignment. Giving birth as well as productiveness is controlled by the hormone of the HPG alignment.

Women who are not acquiring enough caloric intakes to support HPG axis could possibly experience irregular menses; this is with regards to intermittent fasting. Shortened, this insinuates that on condition that a lady lacks sufficient nutritious or breakdown vigor to sustain her during the prenatal period, your (her) body will send signals to your mind to shut down the multiplicative sequence.

Undesirable energy stability or caloric limitation in the undeveloped women may as well have the consequences of adjourning adolescence through impacts on the HPG alignment and neuro-hormones. Absent or irregular menstrual periods are caused by excessive exercise; this is an important piece of information for women. Currently, if you are not thinking about having a baby or getting pregnant at this position in your life, then you should know that your body is. The procreative system within a woman is designed to support the prenatal period right from the time you experience your period until such a period that you stop menstruating, that is menopause. In order to support and maintain a healthy pregnancy, females ought to have certain amounts of energy as well as nutrients, acquired from food and then kept as fats, to be able to support their wellbeing pregnancy. Women's bodies have the capability to distinguish the times these energy stores are down and are able to, in essence 'switch' your procreative sequences so that you do not get pregnant. The means through which this takes place is, in fact, quite intricate and needs a weak sense of balance of signals to be communicated amid the brain, the pituitary glands as well as the ovaries. Characteristically, the time a woman regains heaviness and (or) returns back to a diet rich in nutrients, the usual menstrual sequences will come back.

Various outside and interior contributions of the mind are key rulers of the multiplicative fitness and menstrual sequences.

These contributions can comprise of aspects such as your liveliness condition, your dietary and calories consumption plus spending, constant worry points and also exterior contributions into the heartbeat. Those numerous contributions work via the HPG alignment by influencing the work of "the gonadotropin-releasing hormone (GnRH)". This hormone's role is to be accountable for the discharge of "the follicle-stimulating hormone (FSH)" plus "the luteinizing hormone (LH)" to the blood circulation from the frontal pituitary gland found in a human being's brain. Follicle-stimulating Hormone, in addition, the Luteinizing Hormone, as soon as they are released, move to a woman's ovaries to help the discharge of follicles of the ovary, which comprise of the egg cells, the creation of estrogen plus progesterone as well as testosterone. Gonadotropin-releasing Hormone is seen as a neuro-hormone; therefore, it is secreted from exceptional gonadotropin-releasing hormone neurons found in the brain, precisely the hypothalamus.

Your reproductive health and menstrual cycle can be influenced external factors such as stress, or your expressive and interactive state. Circadian light-dark is similarly another external factor that affects our reproductive health, and we don't often think. Even though a number of women reside in regions that they get approximately twelve days, twelve nights, people tend to have more irregular menstrual cycles when they go through tremendously extended days or tremendously extended nights such as women living in the poles.

For example, The Hypothalamic-Pituitary-Gonadal alignment is competent to adapt and is similarly adjusted by stress hormone communicating with the inclusion corticosterone, from the hypothalamic-pituitary-adrenal (HPA), and this is because procreation and continued existence require to be synchronized and reasonable. Constant worry, together with psychological constant worry, can unhelpfully influence reproduction in a large number of the mammalian kind, not excluding the humans. Due to nervous tension, women are able to experience ovarian cycle disruption, as well as upstream gonadotropin synthesis and secretion.

The physical pressure and the long-lasting pints of cortisol hormone (a type of stress hormone that disrupts the multiplicative sequence) can be decreased concentrated by healthy points of reasonable workout, slumber, and mindfulness. Fasting is complex especially when it is based on the stress points – fasting is over and over again well-thought-out to be an enclosed or "good" worry, like workout, but you can ask yourself, how much can a woman fast without getting her periods affected?

There are no widespread principles or guidelines on how many times one should starve per month, this is because of its problematic nature and relevance of its application, for example, it would be harmless to a woman struggling to come to be pregnant or to stop any menstrual sequence variations. For any woman, there exists a lot of personal unpredictability in menstrual sequences. Despite the fact that reasonable time-limited feeding (about 12-14 hours for each diurnal or fewer) or else in frequent fasting days underneath twenty-four hours are almost certainly harmless, diet excellence, calories consumption and Body Mass Index are expected to regulate the influences of irregular starvation and keto regimes on procreative wellbeing.

When nutrient deficits and prolonged hypoglycemia or low blood sugar is caused by your intermittent fasting practice, it is possible that the hypothalamic, the pituitary and the gonadal axis will be impacted, and interrupt the secretion of the procreative hormones. At hand are some studies in animal reproductions (undeveloped rats) that have advanced the idea that nutritional restriction through alternating fasting might damagingly impact the hypothalamus-hypophyseal-gonadal alignment and then in a similar measure the reproduction. In one of the studies, rats that were starved on a daily basis (one week of human starvation is similar to a day of starving a rat) which results in up to a forty per cent reduction in caloric consumption, went through significant fluctuations in their body mass, estrous cycle, blood sugar, as well as serum estradiol, testosterone, LH levels and GnRH appearance.

How then can Ramadan period on fasting influence menstrual sequences?

As it is described above, some of the factors that have been established to influence menstrual sequences comprise of severe workout, weight loss, and psychological stressors. But then again, some research inquires have found that irregular eating forms, unusually minute concentrations of leptin (connected to liveliness deficiency) and Ramadan observation as some of the subjects that can influence menstruation. In fact, Ramadan fasting including other procedures of irregular fasting are as well dangerous for expectant women, since researchers have exposed alterations in procreative hormones and reduced weight addition in women who starve for the duration of the Ramadan month.

On the other hand, a different study on females with Polycystic Ovary Syndrome (POS) revealed that Ramadan observance through food abstinence could have accommodating moments on the points of anxiety hormone such as cortisol, whereby with restricted impacts on procreative hormone like the "follicle-stimulating hormone" and "luteinizing hormone." These high points the necessity for additional study on the way starvation might affect women in different ways. For instance, weighty or obese women suffering from stimulating matters may position themselves to the benefit of irregular fasting through time-restricted eating, even if it comprises of a sub-optimal eating plan (for instance, evening eating) just like that of Ramadan starving.

During the period of Ramadan Muslim devotes are faced with an observance that requires the refrain from eating from morning to the evening for all period. Such a form of eating pattern may stimulate procreative hormone sequences both unwaveringly but also meanderingly through interference with a heartbeat and sleeping preparations, particularly since refraining from nutrition and drink throughout the day outlines that back up strong circadian paces. It is clearly recognized that menstrual sequences influence the circadian clock and sleep through gender hormones such as estrogen. For instance, daytime paces of melatonin and cortisol hormones transform during the course of the menstrual round. On the backside, disruption of menstrual progression is correlated with the circadian paces. For instance, women who toilet hours during nighttime are more expected to have menstrual irregularities and extended sequences.

Both the change of working environment and irregular estrogen gesturing can also impact the appearance of the 24-hourly CLOCK genetic factor, with downstream insinuations for procreative fitness and also the growth and progression of breast cancer cells. Day by day measures in the multiplication of cells safeguard your body from ardent cancer cells. Quotidian interference aids cancer cells multiply by allowing them to divide "round the clock."

The disruption and alterations of existing biological patterns, as it usually happens in shift jobs, jet lags, sleep deficiency have significant linkage with the disruption of the reproductive function. Such alteration or modification includes reduced conception rates, distorted hormonal discharge rhythms, increased miscarriage numbers, and greater than before danger of breast cancer. Disconcerted hormonal patterns control the appearance of rhythms of the clock genes as a result of the susceptible nature of female health through the desynchronizing of work schedules.

There is still a lot at hand that limits the knowledge and recognition of how precisely the 24-hourpaceinterference impacts menstruation and procreative well-being, even though there is a huge possibility it has to do with alterations in hormone discharge. The ovary gives the impression of having its personal day to day clock; as soon as this clock is available and tuned with diurnal rhythms somewhere else in your body, the multiplicative sequence can rise. But then again, what does recurrent fasting have to do with this situation? Intermittent fasting predominantly time-limited eating may facilitate you uphold healthy circadian measures by nutrient indications, in the condition that nutrient consumption within the standard points of activities (for example, in the day) is upheld.

Alternatively, being otherwise healthy, you may not wish to starve in the course of the twelve hours and consume simply sooner in the sunset, since this might lead to interrupted circadian pulses that may affect the hormone intensities. Denoting that it may for the time being raise the stress levels as well as cortisol but at the end of the day have a constructive, anti-inflammatory outcome if practiced on a regular basis.

DIFFERENT METHODS OF INTERMITTENT FASTING FOR WOMEN OVER 50

As you follow intermittent fasting, it is important that you follow the guidelines as you get started. With those guidelines for women over 50, you can adopt either of the following fasting protocols:

Intermittent Fasting isn't a diet, yet rather a dieting pattern. In less troublesome terms: it's creating a conscious decision to skirt certain meals deliberately.

By fasting and thereafter eating up deliberately, intermittent Fasting, all things considered, infers that you exhaust your calories during a significant window of the day, and choose not to eat sustenance for a greater window of time.

LEANGAINS

Leangains is moreover a kind of intermittent Fasting, for instance, the 5:2 fasting plan and the well-known Eat Stop Eat program. Once in a while, these undertakings are also called "time-constrained empowering." The Leangains program has you "brisk" (not eating) for 16 hours, by then, eating your common proportion of meals in the accompanying 8-hour period.

EAT, STOP, EAT

Eat Stop Eat is a variation of intermittent Fasting, it works, well, like some other intermittent-fasting diet.

There is up 'til now a bit of leeway to fasting for 16 hours, also as there is no certified harm in fasting for 30 hours. The truth is, insofar as you're fasting intermittently while keeping your lifestyle versatile, you're doing Eat, Stop, Eat.

Using the Eat Stop Eat Method as a LONG-TERM method to get lean quickly, and as a way to deal with STAY lean.

By using a versatile intermittent fasting diet as Eat Stop Eat, you, in a general sense, abuse a "metabolic loophole. "Lose fat, keep muscle, all while sitting inert – it doesn't get much less difficult than this! No cooking, no eating, no horrifying over what you eat, or when you will eat.

An average request with respect to Eat Stop Eat is would I have the option to drink juice while I'm fasting, and the proper reaction is no. With eat stop eat method of Fasting, you ought to eat up as pitiful calories as attainable for 24 hours.

The juice is, truly, very high in calories and high in sugar. Exactly when you're doing a juice fast, you're doing is a low-calorie diet using juice; be that as it may, for the Eat Stop Eat purposes, there should be no juice during those 24-hour periods.

20/4

Dissimilar to the Warrior Diet quickly depicted over, the 20:4 Intermittent Fasting protocol utilized by the low-carb network today alternates a protracted fasting period with a customary ketogenic diet.

The long quick enables insulin to remain low for an all-encompassing period.

The "20" in the 20:4 recipe implies you go 20 hours without eating anything, including ketogenic nourishments.

Everything you can have is no-calorie fluids.

The 20-hour quick is known as the fasting window.

The "4" in the 20:4 equation implies you eat an ordinary keto diet during the four sequential hours that you're not fasting.

The 4-hour eating period is known as the meal eating window.

You need not restrain you're eating to simply night times. You can suit your 20 hours of Fasting and 4-hour eating window to accommodate your inclinations, hunger level, and what's happening in your life.

BREAKFAST AND DINNER FAST

Intermittent Fasting can help because your body works contrastingly when "devouring" contrasted with when "fasting":

At the point when you eat a meal, your body puts in a couple of hours handling that nourishment,

During the "fasted express" (the hours where your body isn't expanding or processing any nourishment), your body doesn't have an as of late devoured meal to use as vitality.

24/0

In case you're considering doing your initial 24-hour quick, the initial step is to supplant any carbs from your breakfast. Contingent upon how much finer carbs you've been having in your breakfast for a very long time, it could take some time like in the range of 4 – 12 weeks to reset your body.

This method includes fasting totally for an entire 24 hours. As a rule, it's just done a few times per week. A great many people quick from breakfast to breakfast or lunch to lunch. With this variant of IF, the reactions can be extraordinary, for example, fatigue, cerebral pains, fractiousness, appetite, and low vitality.

If you pursue this method, you should come back to a typical, solid diet on your non-fasting days.

Intermittent Fasting isn't an enchantment pill

Regardless of whether you are doing IF, keto, low carb, high protein, veggie-lover, the Mediterranean diet – and so on – everything comes down to the nature of your calories and how much you're expending.

It's significant to eat a sound, well-adjusted diet while following IF.

As you progress and monitor how you believe, you may decide to build your fasting window continuously.

36 HOUR FAST

A 36-hour speedy suggests that you brisk one entire day. The 36-hour Fasting is the technique by which you snappy over a day or 24 hours.

Fasting for over 24 hours is the spot, all the charm begins. The more you stay in a fasted state and experience imperativeness hardship, the more your body is constrained to trigger it's life span pathways that help to initiate fat stores, support basic microorganisms, and reuse old decimated cell material through the system of autophagy.

All around, it takes, in any occasion, a day to see important signs of autophagy; be that as it may, you can speed it up by eating low carb before starting the snappy, rehearsing on an unfilled stomach, and eating up some homegrown teas that enliven this methodology.

Fasting for 36 hours isn't that irksome. You eat the previous night, don't eat anything close to the start of the day, lunch nor evening, hit the sack in a fasted state, wake up the next day, brisk two or three hours more, and start eating again.

Things that make the Fasting less complex are shining water, mineral water, dull coffee, green tea, and some homegrown teas.

60 HOURS – THE HIMALAYAN FASTING DIET

Brisk for a consistent 60 hours. Fast after dinner on Day 1 and speedy through the fundamental night. Speedy through Day 2 and Day 3. Break rapidly on Day 4. This is difficult to proceed. Consume high-protein, low-carb, high-fat for those 500 calories.

This is brisk that will debilitate your liver of its glycogen stores and immediately move your body into ketosis. This is seen as a critical marker of autophagy - the slowing down of horrible tissue that is identified with prosperity and life span benefits. The most grounded effects of autophagy occur between the underlying 48 hours after glycogen depletion. This is a moved brisk, in any case, should be extraordinarily convincing for life span benefits.

5:2 AND 4:3 METHOD

Intermittent Fasting is an eating method that incorporates customary Fasting.

The 5:2 diet, for the most part, called the 4:3 diet method, generally called The Fast Diet, is, starting at now, the most renowned intermittent fasting diet.

It's known as the 5:2 diet for five days of the week are run of the mill eating days, while the other two limit calories to 500–600 consistently.

Since there are no requirements about which sustenance's to eat yet, rather when you should eat them, this diet is, even more, a lifestyle.

The Most Effective Method to Do The 5:2 Diet

The 5:2 diet is, in all actuality, simple to explain. For five days of the week, you usually eat and don't have to consider restricting calories.

By then, on the other two days, you decline your calorie admission to a fourth of your everyday needs. This is around 500 calories every day for women and 650 for men.

One standard method for masterminding the week is to fast on Mondays and Thursdays, with a couple of little meals, by then, normally eat for the rest of the week.

Accentuate that eating "ordinarily" doesn't mean you can eat anything. In the event that you gorge on lousy sustenance, by then, you in all probability won't lose any weight anymore, and you may even add more weight.

You should eat a comparable proportion of sustenance just as you hadn't been fasting using any and all means.

NOTE: The 5:2 diet incorporates routinely eating for five days out of every week by then binding your calorie admission to 500–600 calories on the other two days.

Therapeutic points of interest of 5:2 Intermittent Fasting

There are very few assessments on the 5:2 diet unequivocally.

There is a lot of focuses on intermittent Fasting when all is said in done, which shows stunning restorative preferences.

One noteworthy bit of leeway is that intermittent Fasting is apparently easier to seek after than interminable calorie control on any occasion for specific people.

Similarly, various assessments have demonstrated that different sorts of intermittent Fasting may inside and out diminishing insulin levels.

The 5:2 diet caused weight loss like ordinary calorie restriction. Likewise, the diet was amazingly ground-breaking at decreasing insulin levels and improving insulin affectability.

A couple of studies have researched the prosperity effects of changed substitute day fasting, which is, in a general sense, equivalent to the 5:2 diet (finally, it's a 4:3 diet).

One randomized controlled assessment in both runs of the mill weight and overweight individuals indicated critical upgrades in the get-together doing 4:3 fasting, appeared differently in relation to the control bundle that ate conventionally.

Following 12 weeks, the fasting gathering had.

- Decreased body weight by in excess of 12 pounds (5 kg).

- Reduced fat mass by 7.8 pounds (3.5 kg), with no change in mass.
- Reduced blood levels of triglycerides by 20%.
- Increased LDL atom size, which is something to be appreciative for.
- Reduced degrees of CRP, a huge marker of irritation.
- Reduced degrees of leptin by up to 40%.

The 5:2 diet may have a couple of great therapeutic points of interest, including weight loss, decreased insulin resistance, and lessened irritation. It may moreover improve blood lipids.

ALWAYS FAT LOSS

This method includes consolidating the Eat-Stop-Eat method, lean increases, and the Warrior Diet in seven days. So, you can start with leangains on one day, by then Eat-Stop-Eat, by then you can have a full cheat day, by then you seek after that with a 36-hour brisk and continue with the rest of the week exchanging the other fasting conventions.

SUBSTITUTING FASTING

Interchange Day Intermittent Fasting:

Interchange day intermittent Fasting is basically fasting each other day for a 24-hour period. For instance, you would usually eat on Monday, speedy Tuesday, eat Wednesday, prompt Thursday, eat Friday, snappy Saturday, and so forth.

This use of intermittent Fasting is the most standard structure used in inquire about inspects, yet from what I have seen, it isn't outstandingly pervasive actually. I've never endeavored exchange day fasting myself, and I don't plan to do in that capacity.

16/8 DAILY FASTING:

Ideally, the snappy should then be broken around early evening or by and by in case you wake up at 6-7 take after great numerous individuals. Nighttimes and evenings are commonly spent in the fed state.

To be very genuine, despite the fact that I simply do a submitted brisk once consistently, I apparently do 16/8 snappy – unexpectedly – 2-3 times for every week generally, since I would prefer not to eat anything until about early afternoon.

LONGER FAST

Long-term Fasting can take a few distinct structures. The most outrageous is a "dry quick," expending nothing by any stretch of the imagination (nourishment or water). This is unquestionably not fitting, as it's exceptionally unsafe to go for over a day or so without drinking. Water fasting means drinking just water yet devouring no calories during the quick. Another method is juice fasting or expending just leafy foods juices. A few people likewise quick on stock, or amazingly low-calorie protein blends.

FOODS TO AVOID

Losing weight requires a lot of sacrifice and perseverance, although the most important thing is to follow a healthy diet that allows you to say goodbye to extra pounds. If you want to lose weight, do not lose the detail of the following foods that are totally prohibited and that you should quickly eliminate from your daily diet.

PROHIBITED FOODS TO LOSE WEIGHT

Sugars

If you are looking to lose some weight, you should not consume any sugar. Sugar is present in foods such as sweets, sugary drinks, jam or fruit juices.

Fats

Saturated fats are totally prohibited in case you are looking to lose a few kilos. That is why you should not consume foods such as sausages, butter or pate.

Fried

Fried foods are other products prohibited in your daily diet. You should avoid batters and products such as croquettes, breaded chicken or fried fish.

Alcohol

Alcohol is a source of calories that contribute nothing and causes the accumulation of fat in the body. That is why you should not drink any alcohol while you want to lose some weight.

Carbs

Foods made from refined flour are totally prohibited if what you want is to lose a few extra pounds of your body.

Ice creams

Although many people believe that they are healthy and perfect foods to drink in the summer, most of them carry a large amount of sugar, which causes enough fat to accumulate in the body. Although it is a product that does not directly fatten, excessive use of salt in meals can cause fluid retention in your body as well as being really harmful to health.

Fruit juices

Most people think that juices are healthy and perfect for the body. The juices have a very large amount of sugar to avoid at all costs if you want to lose a few kilos.

Bread

Bread is a huge source of carbohydrates, so you should moderate your daily consumption. It is advisable to take integral bread since it is much healthier than that made with normal flour.

Dairy Products

Although they also have good properties for the body, dairy products have a high-fat content, so they are not advisable in case you want to lose weight. It is much better to opt for skimmed milk products to avoid part of the fat.

Prepared sauces

Ketchup, mustard, barbecues... There are for all tastes, but all of them are characterized by their fatty nature and being highly caloric. If you also take into account a large amount of added sugars, artificial colors, additives and preservatives they contain, it will be better than discarding your daily diet if you want to lose weight. A good alternative is to make the sauces yourself at home with completely natural ingredients Rich and healthy!

FOODS THAT YOU SHOULD INCLUDE IN YOUR DIET TO LOSE WEIGHT

Just as there are some foods that you should eliminate from your diet if you are looking for weight loss, there are others that are absolutely recommended to achieve that goal. Take note!

Fruits

In addition to providing a large amount of fiber and being rich in vitamins, fruits help improve digestion and lose abdominal fat. Among them, the following are highly recommended:

Apples: the apple is one of the healthiest fruits that exist.

Watermelons: according to several studies carried out, watermelon lowers body fat and lowers cholesterol.

Oranges, lemons, grapefruit, kiwifruit: the vitamin C present in these fruits makes us process fat faster.

Strawberries: they are not very caloric and also contain a lot of fiber and water.

Bananas: Bananas contain satiating properties which will make you eat less. In addition, they are rich in minerals and quality proteins.

Vegetables

Vegetables should be included in every healthy and balanced diet. Within them, the most beneficial are:

Chard, spinach and lettuce: green vegetables act very effectively against abdominal fat.

Celery: Celery is an excellent food that improves digestion and accelerates metabolism, causing us to lose more calories than we gain. 100% recommended!

Tomato: it is a very low-calorie vegetable very suitable for a balanced diet.

Legumes

Some legumes, such as lentils and chickpeas, are ideal for weight loss. They are a source of vegetable protein and help abdominal tone muscles. Of course, it is preferable that you consume them fresh and not canned.

Seafood

Several studies have shown that the monounsaturated fats that seafood contains are perfect for preventing fat accumulation. Still, don't forget to consume it in moderation.

Oatmeal

Highly recommended in diets to lose weight because it contains a high fibre content that absorbs fat and also generates a satiating effect that will make you eat less.

Fish

Fish is rich in vitamins, proteins, minerals and acid grades. To lose weight, enter it in your diet by grilling or baking it.

GOLDEN RULES TO KEEP IN MIND TO LOSE WEIGHT

The experts are clear: to lose weight and maintain it in the long term; the only key is to follow a varied and balanced diet and accompany it with some physical exercise. Do not forget these premises:

Balance and Moderation

The goal of any weight loss plan is to eat fewer calories than the body spends to create a caloric deficit.

Fundamental to Do Sports

Cardiovascular exercises such as fast walking, cycling or running are the most effective at removing excess fat from the body.

Dieting Does Not Mean Starving

The real key is not in quantity but in quality. You should know how to choose well and always opt for those foods that have a low caloric intake.

It's Not About Dieting, But About Changing Habits

It is useless for you to spend three months on a demanding and restrictive regimen if afterwards, you will return to the same inadequate diet as always. If what you want, in addition to losing weight, is to maintain it in the long term, you should not understand the diet as a special way of feeding during a specific period, but as a change of habits for a lifetime.

Compensation Law Applies

If one day you spend on lunch, for example, you can try to eat lighter dinner to compensate and thus not affect the total daily calories.

Don't Skip Meals

The only thing you will get like this is to arrive with a fierce hunger to the next meal and destroy everything. You will get the opposite effect to the desired one!

Dieting does not mean having to give up meetings with friends and family

In most bars and restaurants, they offer light and healthy alternatives such as salads, vegetable dishes, fish or grilled meats...

Enjoy What You Eat

A healthy diet that, at the same time, allows you to lose weight does not have to be boring. Try mixing ingredients, an experiment in the kitchen, create and taste. You will surprise yourself!

NUTRITION GUIDELINES FOR INTERMITTENT FASTING

Intermittent Fasting is low protein and low carbohydrate. At least animal products are allowed. Protein must come from plant sources. Fats should come from healthy vegetable sources such as avocado, olive oil, and coconut oil. Micronutrients complement each other in the form of sea salt.

The Downsides of Intermittent Fasting

Although studies have found promising results using the Intermittent Fasting diet, it may not be for everyone.

Pregnant women and the elderly who are 70 or older should not attempt the Intermittent Fasting.

If you decide you'd like to experience the potential health benefits of the Intermittent Fasting yourself, speak with your physician and a nutritionist first. Be sure not to overdo it. Doing more than one five-day cycle per month could lead to nutrient deficiencies and adverse effects on health. Those should consult a geriatrician before trying the fasting-mimicking diet.

Also, the meal kits for Intermittent Fasting is designed to give people the right ratio of nutrients for their Intermittent Fasting can be a little expensive for some people. However, the cost cannot be compared to the numerous benefits you will get when you do Intermittent Fasting.

Who Should Avoid the Fasting Mimicking Diet?

Intermittent Fasting isn't recommended for specific populations, such as pregnant or breastfeeding women and those who are underweight or malnourished. Also, people with medical conditions, such as diabetes or kidney disease, should only use this plan under the supervision of a doctor.

Intermittent fasting may also not be appropriate for people with a history of eating disorders.

Transitioning into the Intermittent Fasting Lifestyle

I view intermittent fasting as a lifestyle, not a diet, and that includes making healthy food choices whenever you do eat. Intermittent Fasting is most likely safe for healthy women and may provide several health benefits.

Also, proper nutrition becomes more important when fasting, so you want to choose your food before fasting.

This includes minimizing carbohydrates and replacing them with healthy fats such as coconut oil, olive oil, olive oil, butter, eggs, avocado, and nuts. It usually takes several weeks to switch to fat-burning, but once you do, your cravings for unhealthy foods and carbohydrates will disappear automatically.

This is because you can now burn stored fat and no longer need to rely on the new carbohydrates that are consuming. Unfortunately, despite the available evidence, many health professionals are still reluctant to prescribe fasting for their patients.

In addition to eliminating your cravings for sugary snacks and turning it into an efficient fat burner, which makes bodyweight much easier to maintain, modern science has confirmed that there are many other good reasons to switch quickly. Have.

For example, research presented at the annual meetings of the American College of Cardiology in New Orleans showed that fasting increased 1,300 percent of human growth hormone (HGH) in women and 2,000 percent in men.

HGH, a human growth hormone, commonly called "fitness hormone," has a vital role in maintaining health, fitness, and longevity, including promoting muscle growth and increasing fat through metabolism restoration. The fact that this helps build muscle while losing fat simultaneously explains why HGH helps you lose weight without sacrificing muscle mass and why even athletes can benefit from this exercise (provided they are not controlled and nurtured). The only other that can compete with HGH to dramatically increase levels is high-intensity distance training.

MYTHS AND MISCONCEPTIONS

There are so many myths about intermittent fasting circulating in health books and on the Internet. These erroneous statements have created a stigma around intermittent fasting that causes people to avoid following this breakthrough diet. Learn to see through these myths which are not true.

Fasting is Dangerous

This first myth is simply ridiculous. Everyone intermittently fasts as they sleep. Doing it at other times or for a few days on end is no more dangerous than simply fasting while you sleep. The body needs a period to perform autophagy, and it cannot do that if it is too busy processing food all of the time. Intermittent fasting gives your body a well-deserved break while helping you preserve your health.

Remember, fasting is not starvation. You can still eat. Don't confuse fasting, which is healthful with starvation, which is dangerous.

Fasting Can Lower Your Blood Sugar Dangerously

The body can maintain its own blood glucose levels by releasing glycogen, or sugar stored in the liver. This fact means that you won't go low dangerously if you stop eating for a spell. Instead, it will balance out and cause your body to start burning fat. The fat will keep you nourished and prevent fainting from not eating.

If you feel faint or lightheaded, you may need to eat. Be sure to listen to your body. Decrease your fasting period if you keep having dizzy spells.

However, if you are diabetic or hypoglycemic, you may need some help to maintain blood sugars during fasting. Ask your doctor how you can do this maintenance. Some fruit juice will technically break your fast, but it is necessary if your blood glucose plummets down.

It Will Cause Hormonal Imbalance

If anything, IF will balance your hormones. Doing IF wrong will indeed cause leptin and ghrelin, the main hunger hormones, to go crazy and make people binge. Then they will feel guilty and restrict themselves more. The hormones will get even more imbalanced. This effect can suppress a woman's ovulation and even stop her period. However, a woman who implements IF correctly by keeping herself nourished in her eating windows will not experience this at all.

It Will Destroy Your Metabolism

Your metabolism will run on whatever energy source is easiest. Sugar from food is the easiest, so your body burns that first. With no sugar present, the body turns to burn its own fat cells. Either way, your metabolism works. You cannot destroy it.

Some say that if you fast, you will overeat and then have even more trouble losing the weight. This problem is psychological, not physiological. Often people hate restrictive diets so much that they do overeat when they stop dieting, causing them to gain the weight back. Then, they are resistant to new diet approaches and have trouble losing the regained weight. Affecting over 80% of people who have dieted, this problem is pretty common. But if you stick with IF and nourish yourself properly, you won't return to overeating, and you won't have this problem. IF doesn't ruin your metabolism to the point where you can't lose weight again if you do gain any back.

It Causes Stress

Technically, fasting is a period of stress. But as Dr. Fung points out, it is good stress that causes your cells to do their work more efficiently and handle the stress of illness more successfully. Therefore, fasting will not cause extra stress.

The first week or so can be stressful because the approach involves change. Relax a lot and do things you enjoy or find soothing. The stress will pass.

Fasting Can Lead to Overeating

If executed with care, you can avoid the urge to binge eat later. It is true that fasting will make you hungry because of your body's hunger signals. You may feel the urge to eat more when you can or cheat on your fast. The key here is to keep yourself well- nourished when you do eat. Use bone broth to stave off cravings during fasting periods. Also, avoid going on long fasts when you first start. Don't allow the temptation of food around you or have lots of easy snacks in the house as you fast.

Fasting Causes the Body to go into Starvation Mode

Starvation mode is a myth that some people believe causes the body to hold onto weight when it perceives that it is not getting sufficient calories. Look at any person who has starved themselves, and you will see rapid, immediate weight loss and wasting. That picture of starvation proves that restricting calories to dangerous levels will not cause weight gain, but rather weight loss. Plus, fasting is not a dangerous caloric restriction or starvation so it will not cause any unhealthy "mode."

Fasting Causes the Body to Burn Muscle

Because fasting stimulates the production of HGH, it builds muscle rather than destroys it. It only promotes your body to eat fat, not muscle. People tend to start losing muscle mass if they consume too few calories, or essentially starve themselves. But they will not lose muscle if they stay nourished and hydrated and eat well between fasting periods.

You Can't Work Out While Fasting

You can absolutely work out while fasting. If you have eaten well during your eating window and have some extra body fat, exercise will only make your body burn more. Your body will get the nutrition it needs to fuel the workout from your fat stores and the last meal you ate. Be sure to stay hydrated for energy.

DEADLY MISTAKES AND HOW TO AVOID THEM

Fasting is not generally seen as a diet, yet a specific way of life and recommended eating schedule. This type of eating plan has increased enormous notoriety as of late, particularly for women over 50. As we have seen, you may fast for 16 hours and eat during an 8-hour window. This is the 16-8 plan and is commonly seen as the standard intermittent fasting plan. A few people follow the alternate day plan, with low calorie intake on one day and the usual amount the following. Whatever the way you handle it, when your goal is to get in shape, intermittent fasting is famous for one peculiar characteristic: it only works when done correctly.

There are a few potential health benefits when following intermittent fasting. Among the benefits we may include decreased danger of malignant growth, diabetes, and heart disease. Fasting can trigger autophagy, which is known to help with dementia. Regardless of whether you utilize one or another kind of intermittent fasting, it is critical to avoid the traps that can undermine your endeavors. Here below are a few intermittent fasting mistakes a lot of people, especially on their first times, frequently make.

Looking for too Many Improvements too Fastly

You are preparing to begin something new, and you are eager to receive all the rewards as fast as could be. It is just normal that you are excited about this new lifestyle and you want to fully dive into it. Nevertheless, attempting to immediately get such a large number of improvements too early may disrupt your endeavors.

The key is to begin gradually by including a couple of changes one after another. For instance, if you have chosen to do two 500 calorie days every week while having a regular number of calories the other five; consider beginning with only one 500-calorie day. After a couple weeks, you can feel more confident including the second day into your weekly schedule.

Not Taking Care of Your Hydration

Staying in a fasting state can be challenging regardless of whether you are not eating. Most drinks will break the fast and extraordinarily diminish any benefits. Despite the fact that they are fat and calorie free, it is anything but smart to drink "diet" soft drinks. Indeed, even sugars that have zero calories can negatively influence your insulin levels.

The essential fluid you ought to drink during your fast is water. A moderate amount of coffee will not break your fast, but you will need to take your coffee black, in any case. Indeed, even a little sugar in your coffee, like lemon in your water, can influence the fasting period.

Not Drinking Enough Water

While it is crucial not to drink inappropriate fluids when fasting, it is similarly as essential to ensure you drink enough water. Not getting enough water can make you hungry, and it is anything but difficult to sometimes confuse thirst with hunger.

People get a great deal of water from a good part of the foods they eat. Worldwide Food Information states that 20 percent of the water our bodies use originates from food. This implies that in case you are not eating for a few hours you will have to drink around 20 percent more water than usual to compensate for any shortfall.

Eating Unhealthy Foods

Since intermittent fasting is not generally a diet plan, there are not any foods that are "forbidden". This can lead many people to fall into the snare of binge on junk food the moment their fast is up and the eating time opens. Try not to make a habit of unhealthy eating thinking that fasting will compensate for it.

Overeating After Each Fast

This is presumably the greatest trap for both beginners and people who have been fasting intermittently for quite a while. Practicing intermittent fasting to get more fit will lose effectiveness if you end up taking in an excessive number of calories on every chance you have to eat.

One approach to hold back from overeating is to eat larger amounts of healthier foods during your eating window. This would include heaps of healthy plates of mixed greens and crisp vegetables. It is additionally a smart idea to arrange meals and having seasonings prepared before your fast period starts.

Trying to Stick to the Wrong Plan

There are many different approaches to put intermittent fasting into your daily schedule. What works for one person, may not necessarily fit in for another one. To get the most rewards of intermittent fasting, you should take your time to thoroughly analyze different types of plans. It is all right if it takes a little longer to find out the plan that best works for you.

Working Out Too Much or Too Little

It is critical to remain as dynamic as possible, but you would prefer not to overdo, especially during your fasting times. A few newbies may feel overwhelmed, beginning to follow a new eating schedule, and may overlook exercise altogether. Others might be so enthusiastic that they end up overdoing it.

It is a smart thought to pick a moderate exercise schedule, particularly when beginning. Strolling the pooch for twenty minutes or riding your bicycle to work are simple approaches to add moderate exercise to your customary calendar.

Not Drinking Enough Water

Misunderstanding Real Hunger Signs

Perhaps the best thing that I have learned from my intermittent fasting test is that I found a good pace about when appetite shows.

It does not come at 9 am when I've been awake for one hour and last ate a late-night nibble at 11 pm the prior night.

No doubt, your stomach may be growling, and you may desire for something yummy.

Yet, you are not really hungry.

Also, it may be wonderful to binge with your family or friends and enjoy the social part of feasting.

Yet, again, you are not really hungry.

Intermittent fasting will teach you that if you stand by fasting long enough, more often than not, your "hunger" will blur generally in no more than five or ten minutes.

It most likely already happened without you noticing or giving it a particular thought.

How many times at work you were planning to go to eat, then some however, some last-minute rush job showed up, and one hour or two passed by, while you overlooked your stomach's protest?

What before looked like the most urgent priority, eating, was overshadowed by something new that popped up. And you survived!

In any case, yielding and eating too early is one of the serious mix-ups with intermittent fasting. Think that simply drinking some water and allowing it ten minutes or so, you will, usually your appetite will calm down.

Try not to break your intermittent fasting plan before you even begin.

Try not to easily give in to bogus hunger!

Using Intermittent Fasting as an Excuse to Overeat

One of the most harmful intermittent fasting mistakes is give in to the temptation to say, "What the heck, I've starved myself throughout all the day, I deserve to reward myself for supper!", and then diving in a crazy feast of junk food bombing yourself with unhealthy stuff.

Please don't be that woman.

You would feel hopeless, and most likely put on weight.

We don't want that.

In spite of the fact that, actually, intermittent fasting is not a diet because it does not confine what you eat, it is yet critical to settle on healthier food decisions. You want, most of all, to have a healthy relationship with your food and your body.

You can absolutely overeat and put on weight even by eating just once per day, in case you are eating a greater number of calories than your body consumes.

While you do not need to be an absolute stickler and there is space for adaptability, still, be shrewd.

Help yourself out and do not go crazy during your eating window.

Not Eating Enough

If you have yet to attempt intermittent fasting the risk of not eating enough during eating times may appear to be illogical.

Actually, for some people, not eating for a particularly long period of time, it's not unusual to become less hungry.

In some cases, fasting can thoroughly kill your appetite.

Unless you are deliberately doing a total fast (not suggested if not under medical control), however, it is anything but a good idea to decide not to eat enough.

If you should not eat sufficiently for too long, you can easily wreck your digestion and unbalance your hormones.

Moreover, you will deny your body of fundamental nutrients, which can help health avoiding issues that are far more important than the loss of a couple of additional pounds.

Consult your physician about a complete, healthy calorie intake that is fit for weight loss and may help you reach your desired outcomes.

Failing to Plan Your Meals in Advance

While calorie tallying is not important (however truly, you will show more signs of improvement results if you do it), carefully planning and thinking about what you will eat when you're eating period arrives is a great intermittent fasting hack.

This will allow you not to have to improvise when you are finally going to sit down at the table.

Rather than going like "I'm starving and need to eat now no matter what" and then heading to the closest, cheapest, and more unhealthy junk food, you better learn to tell yourself "well, I'm feeling hungry now, but I can wait, I'm not dying and something healthy and delicious is waiting for me, later".

Utilizing this opportunity to consider what you will eat when you eat and sticking to healthier options will only have benefits for you over the long term.

You will learn how to eat for effective weight loss, while decreasing caloric intake, keeping you satisfied, and boosting your self-confidence.

In case you are fasting for 16 hours, you can easily invest 5 minutes of your time to plan what meal will break your fast later.

It is really not unreasonably hard and will prepare for a slimmer future!

Not Exercising at All

While it's true that you actually could, in any case, lose a lot of weight with intermittent fasting even without working out at all, why on earth would you pass up the mind-blowing chance to lose significantly more, faster, and with a bunch of other benefits for your health?

It really has neither rhyme nor reason.

Time will be time. A month is a month. In the event that in one month you could be lazy and shed five pounds or exercise three times a week and lose ten, wouldn't you go for the ten?

SOME PRACTICAL TIPS TO START INTERMITTENT FASTING

The most delicate phase of intermittent fasting is the time when you just start it. That is the time when most people give up on it. If people indeed lose some weight, then they get so excited that they start falling back to their old and unhealthy lifestyles and if they do not get the results they wished for, they too they think that intermittent fasting is a complete waste of time. If you have been doing it for a week and got some results, it is really great and I totally appreciate but in order to reap the full benefits, you need to keep practicing it and make it a lifestyle habit. So, here are some tips that will help you start intermittent fasting the right way.

Break Your Fast with the Right Foods

At the end of a fast, when you eat something after a long time, eating the wrong foods can actually spike up the levels of blood sugar, and so you need to be careful about what you are eating. The same thing happens with the level of insulin in the body because they are never consistent. But intermittent fasting has profound benefits when it comes to lowering the levels of insulin in the body. When there is an elevation in the levels of insulin, that is exactly when the body stops burning fat.

Similarly, if insulin is present in huge quantities in your bloodstream, then it will be highly difficult for your body to burn any fat. Now one of the main aims of engaging in intermittent fasting is so that your body can go into a fat-burning mode. So suppose you have complete an almost perfect fast, but in the end, you break it by consuming the wrong type of food, then all that effort that went into the fast was for nothing and the insulin levels will also start to spike.

So, in order to support the process of fat burning, you need to choose foods that are wholesome, and they should not be processed foods. The insulin levels are very heavily impacted when you consume carbs, so your goal is to stick to foods that are low in carbs. Protein has only a moderate impact but there are certain dairy products that can leave quite the impact. The least amount of impact is left by fats and that is also why the keto diet is encouraged when you are on an intermittent fasting regime.

So, stop indulging in carbs or dairy when you are breaking your fast. Sometimes, people overdo it when they break the fast because they think that they somehow have to compensate for the fasting. But it is not that. Also, you need to remember that you can get carried away easily if you are not focused enough.

Fast for Longer Periods Once You Are Accustomed to the Process

Whenever you fast, the amount of insulin in the blood is lowered. So, that is when the body starts burning fat. Thus, the longer you can fast, the longer you can allow your body to stay in the fat-burning mode. But you should not jump into long fasts right in the beginning. At first, you have to master the protocols mentioned in the short-term fasts, and then you have to move on to the longer ones. Extended hours of fasting can be an entire day, or you can also try out the 48-hour fast once the full day fasting becomes easy.

The advice that I give to every beginner is that you should start with the 16/8 method because in this, you will have to fast for a period of sixteen hours, and if you decide to skip breakfast, then more than half the fasting window is spent sleeping. So, the process becomes quite easier. After you have performed the 16/8 method for about a week or so and you are feeling that it is becoming easy for you, start by doing a 20-hour fast daily. This means that the eating window becomes really short and you have to squeeze it to four hours. Even if the timeframe is short, you can have two small meals here.

Once you have mastered this too, then you can practice the Warrior Diet, which was mentioned at the beginning of this book. In simpler words, you will have only one meal every day. When you have reached the expert level, then you can take your fasts to 36 hours or 48 hours. At first, such long fasting periods will seem impossible and that is perfectly normal. You are not supposed to do it once, but you have to work your way up there. The more you fast consistently, you will notice that the feeling of hunger has started to become blunt. When you are fasting for longer periods, the limitation on calories is increased and fat burning increases too.

Steer Clear of Artificial Drinks

When people are fasting, especially beginners, have this tendency to reach out for the artificial drinks in the form of diet soda, energy drinks, flavored beverages, or even juices. They think that since these drinks claim to have low sugar content, they won't do any harm. But what they don't understand is that these drinks still contain a huge number of artificial sweeteners that can harm your health.

In order to keep your body hydrated, the only liquid that you should have is water. And when you are doing intermittent fasting, there is no limitation to the amount of water you can drink. Some other drinks that are allowed during intermittent fasting are tea and black coffee, but there should be no sugar. You can also have herbal teas, but the criteria remain the same – there should be no milk or sugar in them. These alternatives can easily be swapped in for a soda or other artificial drinks and you can enjoy your fasting windows.

Keep Yourself Busy

This is truly a very truthful tip because if you want your fast to be successful, then you also have to simultaneously keep yourself busy doing something or the other. It can be anything like pursuing a hobby, engaging in your favorite pastime or even work. You can do anything that will involve not thinking about food. This is one of the best ways in which you can adapt to the process of intermittent fasting. In order to be successful with the process, your task is to develop the right mentality and staying will help you with that and this will also make fasts of extended periods bearable.

If you decide to start your fast-post-dinner, then that sorts out most of the problem. Do you know why? It is because the maximum portion of the time will be spent sleeping. That is why beginners are always advised to start their fast-post-dinner. Now, when you are breaking your fast, if you have the meal at around noon, then it can seem quite a long stretch of time to not do anything and sit idle. This is how you will be getting the cravings. So, you need to figure out a way to fill up your mornings so that you can divert your mind from the thought of food. Do some type of productive work. When you are waiting to break your fast with a meal, the last few hours are really crucial and that is also when people lose their patience and break their fast early.

Have Proper Sleep

Whether you are into intermittent fasting or not, sleep will always be essential for you, and it is a universal truth. When you are asleep, your body works to repair your old and worn-out cells. So, sleeping properly is very crucial. You must also know that when you are sleeping, your body burns a certain number of calories which is crucial to your weight loss journey. This also helps in giving a boost to your metabolism. The fat burning process will make your body undergo a lot of changes in the fasting window.

Stay Away from Unsupportive People

When you are starting something new, it is very natural on your part to tell others about it, especially the ones you think you are close to. And then, you also seek their approval on the matter not that it is required but it will simply put your mind at ease. But in most cases, your peers or sometimes even your family members might not like the idea, and they might even reject your ideas. This happens quite often. Think about all those times when you had just started a new venture and you simply couldn't stop yourself from telling it to others. But the moment you speak with someone else, they shoot you down. This can discourage you to great extents, and sometimes, the criticism they state might not even be true.

MEAL-PREPPING TIPS

Getting organized is one of the most vital components of successful meal prep. It may seem daunting or like a waste of time to sit down and organize recipes and write everything out, but it will end up saving you time down the road. The amount of meals you prepare in advance and the amount of time you spend cooking is completely up to you.

Figure Out Your Plan

First, you'll need to design your meal plan. You can plan out a few days, a week, or even the entire month. Find simple recipes and write down everything you'll be eating and at what time. When you're first starting with intermittent fasting and meal planning, the excitement may tempt you to look for fancy, new recipes or a lot of variety, but when you're in the initial stages of a new lifestyle change, one of the most beneficial things you can do is stick to the basics and not complicate things.

Write Your Grocery List

Once you've gotten your recipes together and your meal plan written out, it's time to figure out what you need. Check your refrigerator and your pantry prior to writing your grocery list, so you don't purchase things you already have. After you've compiled a list of things you have on hand, write out a grocery list of the remaining items you'll need to complete your recipes and your meals for the week (or for whatever length of time you've chosen).

You can save even more time by organizing your grocery list based on where items are found in the supermarket. You can list all meats together, all produce items together, and all refrigerated items together. If you need to go to different stores for any deals or any specialty items, organize your lists by store.

Make Your Meals

A great way to save time is to do your shopping on the same day you're going to make your meals. That way, you won't have to put as many grocery items away when you get home, you can jump right into making your meals. Once your meals are cooked, divide them into separate containers by portion sizes and label them appropriately. Now when you're ready to eat, you'll have a meal ready to go, and if you're taking a meal with you on the go, it will be easy to transport.

BURN FAT DOING EXERCISES

When you do the right exercises while practicing the intermittent fasting program, you boost your fat-burning ability by a whopping 74%.

BENEFITS OF EXERCISES

There are many benefits of exercise, such as:

- A higher metabolic rate which aids in fat loss

- It releases endorphins which will make you feel happier

- Prevents muscle atrophy. If you don't use it, you lose it.

- Improves blood circulation

- Prevents diseases that cause cognitive decline

- Encourages better sleep

- Keeps your weight under control

- And much, much more!

EXERCISES THAT BURN THE MOST FAT

Above all, we want to make sure that our exercise program is designed to help us stay fit and healthy and help us burn fat. When you include fattening exercises, you can accelerate your efforts to lose weight.

Exercises that burn fat, even after you finish your workout, will keep your metabolism high for hours, giving you more benefits.

Running or Walking

During exercise, calories burned, and body fat percentage are reduced. Therefore, exercise not only helps you reduce abdominal fat but also helps you lose fat from other areas. Running and walking are two of the best exercises to burn fat.

Also, the only equipment you need is a good pair of shoes. Between the two, running burns more calories, but walking is not far away.

Swimming

Swimming is an excellent way to add strength to the upper body, but it is also an excellent exercise to burn fat. How much you will be surprised when you can navigate for the first time: it is a difficult job. But, with swimming, you will gain resistance.

This is really another great thing about sports. Over time, you can swim faster. To begin, swim for about 15 minutes and add five minutes to each session. You should have a swimming session about three times a week.

Cycling

We all know that cycling can be done at leisure. But, if done with high intensity, it can be a great exercise that burns fat. Travel fast or try mountain biking. You will soon discover that the difference in speed or tone pumps your heart, so this is a great exercise that burns fat.

Cycling can also help build muscle in the legs. This is one of the most natural exercises to help burn fat because you can do it on a standard bicycle outdoors or indoors.

Jumping on a Trampoline

Do not think that the trampoline is only for children. Jumping can increase your heart rate, so it is a great exercise that burns fat. If you move, it can be very intense. It is also said that jumping on the trampoline cleanses the body of toxins through the lymphatic system so that it can improve your immune system in the process. If you don't have an outdoor trampoline, a mini trampoline will also work.

Try to do three sessions a week. Start with five-minute sessions and work up to fifteen or twenty minutes. With this exercise the fat burning will be prolonged a little.

Reverse cut

When you don't know how to lose abdominal fat for women, reverse congestion may be your solution.

> ➢ Lie on the flat floor with your arms together.
> ➢ Cross your legs and lift them off the floor to create a 90-degree angle.
> ➢ Contract your abdominal muscles and lift your head and shoulders off the floor.
> ➢ Return when you sign a contract. Breathe when you go down
> ➢ Perform 1-3 sets with repetition 12-16: vertical crushing of the foot
> ➢ Lie with your hands behind your back.
> ➢ Stretch your legs straight with your knees.
> ➢ Press the Flex abs to lift the head and shoulders from the floor
> ➢ Lie down
> ➢ Keep your feet in the air all the time
> ➢ Exhale when you are flexible
> ➢ Perform set 1-3 with repeat 12-16

Tennis

Tennis keeps you moving and improves your agility. Tennis is an excellent exercise to burn fat because you are always on the move. Play singles instead of doubles to get the best fat burning effect.

Playing tennis three times a week can help burn fat. This will also tie your arms and legs.

Basketball

A fun basketball game may seem like a simple fun event for a Saturday afternoon, but it's also a great fat-burning exercise. Basketball is a fast-paced game that promotes agility. Play with your best friends at least three times a week to get the best results.

Although these are some of the best exercises to burn fat, it is essential to remember that any activity that can keep your heart beating and keeping it there will help you burn fat. Intensity is what matters in fat burning exercises, so as long as your heart pumps and continues to sweat, you will be in the training area!

It may require a Herculean effort to go from a sedentary lifestyle to an active one. The key here is small improvements daily. If you've not been exercising for years, you can start with a 20-minute walk daily.

Do not jump into a high-intensity workout overnight. Give your body time to adapt and recover. Start with low impact exercises such as walking, cycling, and swimming. Then move on to resistance training with light weights.

There is no need to train to the point of exhaustion when you're starting. What matters is that you move more and get into the habit of exercising regularly. Over time, you can increase the intensity of your workouts and challenge yourself.

Do note that it is ok to train on an empty stomach, but it is preferable that within 45 minutes from completion of your workout, you should have a meal. So, you could either train during your eating window or start your eating window after your workout.

BREAKFAST RECIPES

1. OMELET WITH PEPPERS

Preparation Time: 10 minutes

Cooking Time: 15 minutes

Servings: 4

INGREDIENTS

- 4 eggs, beaten
- 1 tablespoon margarine
- 1 cup bell peppers, chopped
- 2 oz scallions, chopped

DIRECTIONS

1. Toss the margarine in the skillet and melt it.
2. In the mixing bowl mix up eggs and bell peppers. Add scallions.
3. Pour the egg mixture in the hot skillet and roast the omelet for 12 minutes.

NUTRITION: Calories per serving: 102 Carbohydrates: 7.3g Protein: 6.1g Fat: 10 .8g Sugar: 3g Sodium: 98mg Fiber: 0.8g

2. QUINOA HASHES

Preparation Time: 10 minutes

Cooking Time: 25inutes

Servings: 2

INGREDIENTS

- 3 oz quinoa
- 6 oz water
- 2 potatoes, grated
- 1 egg, beaten
- 1 tablespoon avocado oil
- 1 teaspoon chives, chopped

DIRECTIONS

1. Cook quinoa in water for 15 minutes.
2. Heat up avocado oil in the skillet.
3. Then mix up all remaining ingredients in the bowl. Add quinoa and mix up well.
4. Add quinoa hash browns, cook for 5 minutes on each side.

NUTRITION: Carbohydrates: 5.9g Calories Per Serving: 344. Protein: 12.5.g Fat: 5.9g Sugar: 0.2g Sodium: 388mg Fiber: 3.4g

3. ARTICHOKE EGGS

Preparation Time: 5 minutes

Cooking Time: 20 minutes

Servings: 4

INGREDIENTS

- 5 eggs, beaten

- 2 oz low-fat feta, chopped
- 1 yellow onion, chopped
- 1 tablespoon canola oil
- 1 tablespoon cilantro, chopped
- 1 cup artichoke hearts, canned, chopped

DIRECTIONS

1. Grease 4 ramekins with the oil.
2. Mix up all remaining ingredients and divide the mixture between prepared ramekins.
3. Bake the meal at 380F for 20 minutes.

NUTRITION: Calories per serving: 177.Carbohydrates: 7.4g Protein: 10.6g Fat: 12.2g Sugar: 1g Sodium: 259mg Fiber: 2g

4. QUINOA CAKES

Preparation Time: 10 minutes

Cooking Time: 25 minutes

Servings: 4

INGREDIENTS

- 7 oz quinoa
- 1 cup cauliflower, shredded
- 1 cup of water
- ½ cup vegan parmesan, grated
- 1 egg, beaten
- 1 tablespoon olive oil
- ½ teaspoon ground black pepper

DIRECTIONS

1. Mix up the quinoa with the cauliflower, water, and ground black pepper, stir, bring to a simmer over medium heat and cook for 15 minutes/
2. Cool the mixture and add parmesan and the eggs, stir well, shape medium cakes out of this mix.
3. Heat up a pan with the oil over medium-high heat, add the quinoa cakes. Cook them for 4-5 minutes per side.

NUTRITION: Calories per serving: 280.Carbohydrates: 6.8g Protein: 25.4g Fat: 7.6g Sugar: 1.2g Sodium: 222mg Fiber: 1g

5. BEAN CASSEROLE

Preparation Time: 10 minutes

Cooking Time: 30 minutes

Servings: 8

INGREDIENTS

- 5 eggs, beaten
- ½ cup bell pepper, chopped
- 1 cup red kidney beans, cooked
- ½ cup white onions, chopped
- 1 cup low-fat mozzarella cheese, shredded

DIRECTIONS

1. Spread the beans over the casserole mold. Add onions and bell pepper.
2. Add the eggs mixed with the cheese.
3. Bake the casserole 380 F for 30 minutes.

NUTRITION: Calories per serving: 142.Carbohydrates: 16g Protein: 23.8g Fat: 3g Sugar: 0.2g Sodium: 162mg Fiber: 2.3g

LUNCH RECIPES

6. CHERRY CHICKEN LETTUCE WRAPS

Preparation Time: 15 minutes

Cooking Time: 10 minutes

Servings: 1

INGREDIENTS

- 12 lettuce leaves
- 2 tbsp canola oil, separated
- ⅓ cup sliced almonds, toasted
- 1 ¼ lb chicken breast, the skin and bones removed and minced
- ½ cup green onion, diced
- 1 tbsp fresh ginger root, thinly cut
- 1 ½ cups carrots, roughly cut
- 2 tbsp rice vinegar
- 1 lb dark sweet cherries, cut in halves and the pits removed
- 2 tbsp teriyaki sauce
- 1 tbsp honey

DIRECTIONS

1. Set your stove to medium high heat and place a large sized skillet on it. Add 1 tbsp of oil to the pan and let it get hot. Put the skinless and boneless chicken in the pot and add your ginger. Saute for

10 minutes. Be careful not to burn your chicken. You just want to make sure it is cooked through.

2. Get a bowl and add honey, vinegar, 1 tbsp oil, and teriyaki sauce. Using a whisk, mix these ingredients well, before throwing in your almonds, the chicken mixture in your skillet, green onion, cherries and carrots.

3. Using a spoon, place the mixture in the center of each of the twelve lettuce leaves. Roll the lettuce to cover this filling, and they are ready to serve.

NUTRITION: Calories per serving: 297.Carbohydrates: 21.5g Protein: 25g Fat: 12.4g Sugar: 2g Sodium: 156mg Fiber: 1g

7. EASY KOREAN BEEF

Preparation Time: 10 minutes

Cooking Time: 10 minutes

Servings: 4

INGREDIENTS

- 1 tbsp sesame seeds
- 2 tsp sesame oil
- 2 tbsp green onion, diced
- 1 lb lean ground beef
- 2 cups cauliflower rice
- 3 garlic cloves, thinly cut
- ¼ tsp ground black pepper
- ¼ cup soy sauce

- ¼ tsp ground ginger
- 1 tbsp coconut sugar

DIRECTIONS

1. Make sure your stove is set to medium high heat and place a large skillet on it. Pour the sesame oil in the pan to make it hot, before adding garlic and ground beef. After 7 minutes, by which time the beef would crumble easily, turn down the stove to low and quickly continue with the next step.

2. Grab a bowl and throw your black pepper, soy sauce, ginger, and coconut sugar in it. Using a whisk, mix these ingredients properly. Now, you can pour the coconut sugar mixture over the cooked beef that is still in the pan. Increase the heat back to medium and let the beef mixture simmer for about 3 minutes.

3. Serve the keto Korean beef on top of your prepared cauliflower rice. Finally, garnish with sesame seeds and green onions.

NUTRITION: Calories per serving: 297.Carbohydrates: 8.9g Protein: 22.4g Fat: 13.3g Sugar: 0.6g Sodium: 956mg Fiber: 3.7g

8. PEANUT SESAME SHIRATAKI NOODLES

Preparation Time: 20 minutes

Cooking Time: 10 minutes

Servings: 4

INGREDIENTS

- 1 8 oz pack shirataki noodles
- 2 tbsp creamy peanut butter
- Snow peas
- 1 tbsp water
- 1 medium carrot, shredded
- 1 tbsp soy sauce, low sodium
- Peanuts
- 1 tsp rice vinegar
- Toasted sesame seeds
- Pinch garlic powder
- Green onions
- ¼ tsp black pepper
- Cilantro
- 1 tsp brown sugar
- Pinch ground ginger
- ⅛ tsp sesame oil

DIRECTIONS

Pasta

1. Grab a medium sized bowl and put the ground ginger, peanut butter, sesame oil, water, brown sugar, soy sauce, black pepper, rice vinegar, and garlic powder inside it. Mix properly and set the bowl aside for 30 minutes.
2. Next, pop that bowl in the refrigerator until you have to use it on the pasta.

To prepare the pasta

3. Rinse your shirataki noodles. Follow that by draining the noodles and patting them dry using a paper towel.
4. Get a nonstick pan and place it over medium low heat. The pan has to be completely dry before the noodles. The purpose of this is to further make sure that the noodles are not wet. Do not burn them.
5. Chop your snow peas and add them, along with the grated carrots, into the pan containing your noodles. Saute for about 4 minutes before you pour the sauce in. Mix the sauce into the other ingredients well.
6. Decorate with cilantro, toasted sesame seeds, green onions, and peanuts. Alternatively, you can choose to not garnish the meal.

NUTRITION: Calories per serving: 111.Carbohydrates: 9g Protein: 12.6g Fat: 6.5g Sugar: 1.9g Sodium: 564mg Fiber: 2g

9. GINGER ASIAN SLAW

Preparation Time: 15 minutes

Cooking Time: 0 minutes

Servings: 8

INGREDIENTS

- Sea salt to your preferred taste
- 6 cups Napa cabbage, minced
- Pepper to your preferred taste
- 6 cups red cabbage, minced
- 3 tbsp lime juice
- 2 cups carrots grated
- 1 medium lime zest
- 1 cup cilantro, shredded
- ¼ tsp cayenne pepper
- ¾ cup diced green onions
- 1 garlic clove, thinly cut
- 1 tbsp extra virgin olive oil
- 1 ½ inch ginger, shredded
- 1 tbsp maple syrup
- 2 tbsp almond butter
- 1 tsp sesame oil
- 1 tbsp rice vinegar
- 1 tbsp apple cider vinegar
- 2 tbsp tamari

DIRECTIONS

1. Into the cup of a blender add your olive oil, salt, pepper, maple syrup, lime juice, sesame oil, lime zest, apple cider vinegar, cayenne pepper, tamari, garlic rice vinegar, ginger, and almond butter. Blend these ingredients until you are left with a smooth mixture. This is your dressing.

2. Next, you'll need a large mixing bowl. Put the cilantro, cabbage, green onions, and carrots inside it. Pour the mixture in your blender into the bowl and toss well.

3. For about an hour, let the bowl stay in your fridge. The various flavors will meld deliciously and afterwards, you can serve.

NUTRITION: Calories per serving: 144.Carbohydrates: 12g Protein: 24.4g Fat: 6gSugar: 1.7g Sodium: 432mg Fiber: 1.7g

10. ZUCCHINI CREAM

Preparation Time: 10 minutes

Cooking Time: 25 minutes

Servings: 8

INGREDIENTS

- 4 cups vegetable stock
- 2 tablespoons olive oil
- 2 sweet potatoes, peeled and cubed
- 8 zucchinis, chopped
- 2 onions, peeled and chopped
- 1 cup coconut milk
- A pinch of salt and black pepper
- 1 teaspoon dried rosemary
- 4 tablespoons fresh dill, chopped
- ½ teaspoon fresh basil, chopped

DIRECTIONS

1. Heat a pot with the oil over medium heat, add the onion, stir, and cook for 2 minutes. Add the zucchinis and the rest of the ingredients except the milk and dill, stir and simmer for 20 minutes.
2. Add the milk and dill, puree the soup using an immersion blender, stir, ladle into soup bowls and serve.

NUTRITION: Calories per serving: 324.Carbohydrates: 10g Protein: 14.8g Fat: 3g Sugar: 1.8g Sodium: 585mg Fiber: 0.4g

DINNER RECIPES

11. PORK BELLY CASSEROLE

Preparation Time: 5 minutes

Cooking Time: 25 minutes

Servings: 4

INGREDIENTS

- 8 pork belly slices, cut into small pieces
- 3 large onions, chopped
- 4 tablespoons lemon
- Juice of 1 lemon
- Seasoning as you needed

DIRECTIONS

1. Take a large pressure cooker and place it over medium heat.
2. Add onions and sweat them for 5 minutes.
3. Add pork belly slices and cook until the meat browns and onions become golden.
4. Cover with water and add honey, lemon zest, sunflower seeds, pepper, and close the pressure seal.
5. Pressure cook for 40 minutes.
6. Serve and enjoy with a garnish of fresh chopped parsley if you prefer.

NUTRITION: Calories per serving: 753.Carbohydrates: 23g Protein: 36g Fat: 4g Sugar: 0g Sodium: 312mg Fiber: 0g

12. FASCINATING SPINACH AND BEEF MEATBALLS

Preparation Time: 10 minutes

Cooking Time: 20 minutes

Servings: 4

INGREDIENTS

- ½ cup onion
- 4 garlic cloves
- 1 whole egg
- ¼ teaspoon oregano
- Pepper as needed
- 1-pound lean ground beef
- 10 ounces spinach

DIRECTIONS

1. Preheat your oven to 375 degrees F.
2. Take a bowl and mix in the rest of the ingredients and using your hands, roll into meatballs.
3. Transfer to a sheet tray and bake for 20 minutes.
4. Enjoy!

NUTRITION: Calories per serving: 200.Carbohydrates: 5g Protein: 29g Fat: 3g Sugar: 3g Sodium: 514mg Fiber: 1g

13.   JUICY AND PEPPERY TENDERLOIN

Preparation Time: 10 minutes

Cooking Time: 20 minutes

Servings: 4

INGREDIENTS

- 2 teaspoons sage, chopped
- Sunflower seeds and pepper
- 2 1/2 pounds beef tenderloin
- 2 teaspoons thyme, chopped
- 2 garlic cloves, sliced
- 2 teaspoons rosemary, chopped
- 4 teaspoons olive oil

DIRECTIONS

1. Preheat your oven to 425 degrees F.
2. Take a small knife and cut incisions in the tenderloin; insert one slice of garlic into the incision.
3. Rub meat with oil.
4. Take a bowl and add sunflower seeds, sage, thyme, rosemary, pepper and mix well.
5. Rub the spice mix over tenderloin.
6. Put rubbed tenderloin into the roasting pan and bake for 10 minutes.
7. Lower temperature to 350 degrees F and cook for 20 minutes more until an internal thermometer reads 145 degrees F.

8. Transfer tenderloin to a cutting board and let sit for 15 minutes; slice into 20 pieces and enjoy!

NUTRITION: Calories per serving: 490.Carbohydrates: 1g Protein: 24g Fat: 9g Sugar: 0g Sodium: 408mg Fiber: 1.7g

14. PEANUT SESAME SHIRATAKI NOODLES

Preparation Time: 20 minutes

Cooking Time: 10 minutes

Servings: 4

INGREDIENTS

- 1 8 oz pack shirataki noodles
- 2 tbsp creamy peanut butter
- Snow peas
- 1 tbsp water
- 1 medium carrot, shredded
- 1 tbsp soy sauce, low sodium
- Peanuts
- 1 tsp rice vinegar
- Toasted sesame seeds
- Pinch garlic powder
- Green onions
- ¼ tsp black pepper
- Cilantro
- 1 tsp brown sugar

- Pinch ground ginger
- ⅛ tsp sesame oil

DIRECTIONS

Pasta

1. Grab a medium sized bowl and put the ground ginger, peanut butter, sesame oil, water, brown sugar, soy sauce, black pepper, rice vinegar, and garlic powder inside it. Mix properly and set the bowl aside for 30 minutes.
2. Next, pop that bowl in the refrigerator until you have to use it on the pasta.

To prepare the pasta

3. Rinse your shirataki noodles. Follow that by draining the noodles and patting them dry using a paper towel.
4. Get a nonstick pan and place it over medium low heat. The pan has to be completely dry before the noodles. The purpose of this is to further make sure that the noodles are not wet. Do not burn them.
5. Chop your snow peas and add them, along with the grated carrots, into the pan containing your noodles. Saute for about 4 minutes before you pour the sauce in. Mix the sauce into the other ingredients well.

6. Decorate with cilantro, toasted sesame seeds, green onions, and peanuts. Alternatively, you can choose to not garnish the meal.

NUTRITION: Calories per serving: 111.Carbohydrates: 9g Protein: 12.6g Fat: 6.5g Sugar: 1.9g Sodium: 564mg Fiber: 2g

15. GINGER ASIAN SLAW

Preparation Time: 15 minutes

Cooking Time: 0 minutes

Servings: 8

INGREDIENTS

- Sea salt to your preferred taste
- 6 cups Napa cabbage, minced
- Pepper to your preferred taste
- 6 cups red cabbage, minced
- 3 tbsp lime juice
- 2 cups carrots grated
- 1 medium lime zest
- 1 cup cilantro, shredded
- ¼ tsp cayenne pepper
- ¾ cup diced green onions
- 1 garlic clove, thinly cut
- 1 tbsp extra virgin olive oil
- 1 ½ inch ginger, shredded
- 1 tbsp maple syrup
- 2 tbsp almond butter

- 1 tsp sesame oil
- 1 tbsp rice vinegar
- 1 tbsp apple cider vinegar
- 2 tbsp tamari

DIRECTIONS

1. Into the cup of a blender add your olive oil, salt, pepper, maple syrup, lime juice, sesame oil, lime zest, apple cider vinegar, cayenne pepper, tamari, garlic rice vinegar, ginger, and almond butter. Blend these ingredients until you are left with a smooth mixture. This is your dressing.

2. Next, you'll need a large mixing bowl. Put the cilantro, cabbage, green onions, and carrots inside it. Pour the mixture in your blender into the bowl and toss well.

3. For about an hour, let the bowl stay in your fridge. The various flavors will meld deliciously and afterwards, you can serve.

NUTRITION: Calories per serving: 144.Carbohydrates: 12g Protein: 24.4g Fat: 6g Sugar: 1.7g Sodium: 432mg Fiber: 1.7g

DESSERT RECIPES

16.   RED VELVET CUPCAKES

Preparation Time: 15 minutes

Cooking Time: 25 minutes

Servings: 8

INGREDIENTS

Cupcake batter:

- 2 cups of almond flour.
- 2 tablespoons of Dutch cocoa.
- 3 tablespoons of butter.
- 1/3 cup of monk fruit/erythritol blend.
- 3 eggs.
- 1/2 cup of sour cream.
- 1/3 cup of buttermilk.
- 2 teaspoon of red food coloring.
- 1 teaspoon of baking powder

Icing

- 1/2 stick butter.
- 2 tablespoon of mascarpone cheese.
- 8 oz. of cream cheese.
- 1/4 cup of monk fruit sweetener.
- 1 teaspoon of vanilla.

DIRECTIONS

1. Using a large mixing bowl, add in the flour, cocoa, and baking powder then mix properly to combine. In another mixing bowl, add in the butter,

sweetener, and eggs then beat properly with a stand mixer. Add in the sour cream, buttermilk, and red coloring then beat again to combine.

2. Next, pour the egg mixture into the bowl containing the flour mixture then stir everything to combine. Place parchment paper on a multi-well muffin tin, pour in the batter, place the muffin tin into an oven and bake at 350 degrees F for about twenty-five to thirty minutes until an inserted toothpick comes out clean, set aside to cool.

3. To make the icing, beat all its ingredients in a mixing bowl until the mixture becomes smooth. ice the cupcakes as desired then serve.

NUTRITION: Calories per serving: 377.Carbohydrates: 5.5g Protein: 7.4g Fat: 24g Sugar: 2.2g Sodium: 345mg Fiber: 2.5g

17. CHOCOLATE PIE DELIS

Preparation Time: 30 minutes

Cooking Time: 15 minutes

Servings: 8

INGREDIENTS

For the crust

- 2 cups of toasted almond flour.
- 8 tablespoons of melted butter.
- 2 tablespoons of unsweetened cocoa.
- 1 teaspoon of organic ground coffee.

- 1 teaspoon of vanilla extract.
- 8 drops of liquid stevia.
- 2-4 tablespoons of powdered monk fruit sweetener.

Filling

- 3 ounces of cream cheese.
- 2 tablespoons of sour cream.
- 2 tablespoons of grass-fed butter.
- 1 tablespoon + 1 teaspoon of vanilla extract.
- 1/2 cup + 2 teaspoons of powdered monk fruit.
- 1/2 cup of unsweetened cocoa powder.
- 1 cup of heavy whipping cream.
- 1/8 teaspoon of almond extract.
- 8 drops of liquid stevia.

DIRECTIONS

1. To make the crust, preheat the oven to 350 degrees F, grease a pie pan with coconut oil then set aside. Using a mixing bowl, add in the flour, butter, cocoa, ground coffee, vanilla extract, stevia, and monk fruit sweetener then mix everything properly to combine with a spatula.

2. Place the crust mixture into the greased pie pan, press out the mixture to evenly distribute in the pan, place the pan into the pleathered oven and bake the crust for about eighteen minutes, set aside.

3. For the pie, using a large mixing bowl, add in the cream cheese, butter, sour cream, 1 tablespoon of vanilla, 1/2 cup of powdered monk fruit, and cocoa powder then mix properly to combine. Use

a hand mixer to mix again until the mixture becomes fluffy and combined.

4. Using another mixing bowl, add in the whipping cream, 2 teaspoons of monk fruit, 1 teaspoon of vanilla, almond extract, and stevia then mix with a hand mixer until peaks form. Pour the cream mixture into the bowl with the cocoa mixture then mix everything to combine.

5. Add the mixture into the prepared crust, then place the pie into the refrigerator to firm up. Slice the pie and serve.

NUTRITION: Calories per serving: 268.Carbohydrates: 4.5g Protein: 2.4g Fat: 6.4g Sugar: 1.7g Sodium: 254mg Fiber: 2g

18.   COFFEE CAKE

Preparation Time: 40 minutes

Cooking Time: 20 minutes

Servings: 4

INGREDIENTS

Coffee Cake

- 3 cups of almond flour.
- 1/4 cup of stevia.
- 1/2 tablespoons of baking powder.
- 1/2 teaspoons of ground cinnamon.
- 1 teaspoon of sea salt to taste.
- 1/4 teaspoon of baking soda.
- 1/4 teaspoon of nutmeg.

- 1/2 cup (1 stick) of melted butter.
- 1 cup of sour cream.
- 2 eggs.

Streusel Topping

- 2 cups of almond flour.
- 1/2 cup of coconut flour.
- 1/2 cup of stevia.
- 1/2 cup of pecans or walnuts.
- 1/2 cup (1 stick) sliced butter.
- 2 teaspoons of ground cinnamon.
- 1/4 teaspoon of sea salt to taste.

DIRECTIONS

1. Preheat the oven to 350 degrees F, grease a cake pan with butter then set aside. For the topping, using a mixing bowl, add in the stevia, flours, pecan nuts, cinnamon, and salt to taste then mix to combine. Add in the sliced butter then mix until the mixture becomes a coarse crumb, set aside.

2. For the cake, mix the flour, stevia, spices, baking powder, baking soda, sea salt to taste then mix properly to combine. In another bowl, add in the melted butter, sour cream, and eggs then mix properly to combine. Pour the mixture into the bowl containing the flour mixture then mix everything to combine.

3. Place the batter into a springform pan, place the topping over the cake batter, place the pan into the preheated oven and bake the cake for about

forty-five minutes to one hour until the cake becomes brown in color and baked through.

4. Once baked, let the cake cool for a few minutes, slice, and serve.

NUTRITION: Calories per serving: 283.Carbohydrates: 7.1g Protein: 5.9g Fat: 28.5g Sugar: 1g Sodium: 1254mg Fiber: 1g

19. DELICIOUS BROWNIES

Preparation Time: 10 minutes

Cooking Time: 20 minutes

Servings: 8

INGREDIENTS

- 1/2 cup of almond flour.
- 1/4 cup of cocoa powder.
- 3/4 cup of erythritol.
- 1/2 teaspoon of baking powder.
- 1 tablespoon of instant coffee which is optional.
- 2 tablespoons of butter.
- 1 oz. of dark chocolate.
- 3 eggs.
- 1/2 teaspoon of vanilla extract which is optional.

DIRECTIONS

1. Preheat the oven to 350 degrees F, place a parchment paper on a baking pan then grease properly with butter, set aside. Using a mixing bowl, add in the flour, cocoa powder, baking powder, erythritol, and coffee then whisk properly to combine. Place a skillet pan over medium heat,

add in the chocolate and butter then melt for a few minutes.

2. Take the chocolate mixture out of the heat, add in the egg and vanilla then whisk properly to combine. Add in the flour mixture then mix again to combine. Pour the batter into the prepared baking pan, place the pan into the preheated oven and bake the brownies for about eighteen to twenty minutes until baked through.

3. Once baked, let the brownies cool in the fridge for about thirty minutes to two hours, slice and serve.

NUTRITION: Calories per serving: 490.Carbohydrates: 3g Protein: 2g Fat: 11g Sugar: 2.2g Sodium: 564mg Fiber: 0g

20. CHOCOLATE CHIP COOKIES

Preparation Time: 10 minutes

Cooking Time: 12 minutes

Servings: 8

INGREDIENTS

- 1 egg.
- 1/2 cup of Swerve sweetener.
- 1/3 cup of organic coconut oil.
- 1 teaspoon of pure vanilla extract.
- 1 1/2 cups of blanched almond flour.
- 1/2 teaspoon of baking soda.
- 1/4 teaspoon of sea salt to taste.
- 1/2 cup of dark chocolate chips.

DIRECTIONS

1. Preheat the oven to 325 degrees F, place a parchment paper on a baking sheet then set aside. using a large mixing bowl, add in the egg and sweetener then whisk properly to combine. Add in the oil and vanilla then whisk again to combine. Add in the flour, baking soda, and salt to taste then mix properly to combine until there is a formation of a dough.

2. Next, fold in the chocolate chips, use a cookie scoop to form cookie shapes out of the dough then place them into the prepared baking sheet. Place the baking sheet into the preheated oven and bake the cookies for about ten to twelve minutes until they become light brown in color.

3. Once baked, let the cookies cool for a few minutes then serve.

NUTRITION: Calories per serving: 129.Carbohydrates: 5g Protein: 1g Fat: 2g Sugar: 1.2g Sodium: 654mg Fiber: 1g

21. CHOCOLATE MOUSSE

Preparation Time: 10 minutes

Cooking Time: 0 minutes

Servings: 10

INGREDIENTS

- 3 ounces of softened cream cheese.
- 1/2 cup of heavy cream.

- 1 teaspoon of vanilla extract.
- 1/4 cup of powdered Swerve.
- 2 tablespoons of cocoa powder.
- 1 pinch of salt to taste.

DIRECTIONS

1. Using a large mixing bowl, add in the cream cheese then beat with an electric mixer until it becomes light and fluffy. Add in the heavy cream and vanilla extract then beat on a low setting. Add in the swerve, cocoa powder, and salt to taste then beat until everything is incorporated.

2. Mix again for about one to two minutes on a high setting until the mixture becomes light and fluffy. Serve.

NUTRITION: Calories per serving: 373.Carbohydrates: 6.9g Protein: 8.4g Fat: 6.9g Sugar: 0g Sodium: 865mg Fiber: 2g

7 DAY INTERMITTENT FASTING FOR WOMEN OVER 50 MEAL-PLAN

Meal Plan	Breakfast	Lunch	Dinner	Dessert
DAY-1	Bean Casserole	Zucchini Cream	Fascinating Spinach and Beef Meatballs	Chocolate pie delis
DAY-2	Quinoa Hashes	Ginger Asian Slaw	Peanut Sesame Shirataki Noodles	Red velvet Cupcakes
DAY-3	Artichoke Eggs	Easy Korean Beef	Ginger Asian Slaw	Coffee Cake
DAY-4	Quinoa Cakes	Peanut Sesame Shirataki Noodles	Juicy and Peppery Tenderloin	Chocolate Mousse
DAY-5	Omelet with Peppers	Cherry Chicken Lettuce Wraps	Pork Belly Casserole	Delicious brownies

| DAY-6 | Quinoa cakes | Easy Korean Beef | Ginger Asian Slaw | Chocolate chip cookies |
| DAY-7 | Bean Casserole | Beef Satay with vegetables | Peanut Sesame Shirataki Noodles | Coffee cake |

CONCLUSION

Before you begin intermittent fasting, you must understand the concept of fasting. Most people relate it to hunger and keep the stomach empty for long hours. It is a significant fact that fasting is not just about keeping the stomach empty or starving for no reason. In some parts of the world, people fast as a religious obligation, while some of them use it as a method of being in shape and losing weight.

Studies show that for a better health standard it is necessary for a person to keep the stomach empty for about 10 to 12 hours. It helps a person to use all body fats and ensure that the energy is fully used. In general, we cannot touch the empty stomach because we take the meals after intervals. At these intervals our food cannot properly digest and burn in the body.

During the fast, things are very different and change. When a person traps for nearly 12 hours, he burns the stored fuel inside. It helps to hit the total empty stomach and uses some extra fuel from the reserves. In general, it is useful to have a balanced and attractive body.

It is a remarkable fact that fasting is not an arbitrary act that you can do alone. A systematic procedure must be designed according to a pattern. The use of patterns helps a person to achieve the right results. In the event that you start random fasting, you will face the consequences, not the result for the effort. So, make sure you have sufficient knowledge about the fast, the techniques and other important details.

Intermittent fasting becomes a trendy way to lose weight. It is considered the best way to lose weight in a short time. In addition, it also improves metabolism and even extends the lifespan. The most amazing part of intermittent fasting is that it has few methods. You can choose the one that suits you.

Losing weight is now no problem. You just have to make a decision and need some courage. Select a method from the intermittent fasting methods. Because all methods are effective, and you get promising results.

Intermittent fasting is an eating schedule. It varies between eating and fasting. You set a period of food according to your purpose. After setting the eating time, stick to it. You only eat while eating and you are stuck for the rest of the hours. In other words, it's a diet.

In the past it was used to heal patients with obesity, diabetes and epilepsy. Now it is used to lose weight. It is a healthy way to help your body function better.

If you are looking for a guide for every type of food, you can cook and to eat to avoid following an intermittent diet you should have this cookbook in your collection.

You just have to read carefully and follow all the advice dedicated to you!